Also by Toni Thomas:

Chosen
Fast as Lightening
Walking on Water
Blue Halo
Ace Raider of the Unfathomable Universe
You'll be Fast as Lightening Coveting my Painted Tail
Hotsy Totsy Ballroom
Love Adrift in the City of Stars
In the Pink Arms of the City
In the Kingdom of Longing
The Things We Don't Know
In the Boarding House for Unclaimed Girls
They Became Wing Perfect and Flew
Unburdened Kisses
Bandits Come and Remove Her Body in the Night
There is This
Here
The Smooth White Vanishing
Perishing in the Rain
A Different Measure of Moonlight
The Secret Language of River
Inside Her a River of Snow was Traveling
Paradise on a Shoestring
A Bride of Amazement

The Arbiter of Her Own Flame

Published 2025
Annalese Press
West Yorkshire HD9 3XZ
England

Copyright © 2008 Toni Thomas

All rights reserved. No part of this publication may be reproduced, stored, or transmitted in any form, or by any means electronic, mechanical or photocopying, recording or otherwise, without the express written permission of the publisher.

Layout and Cover design by Peter Wadsworth
The Bride, Gertrude Kasebier, 1902

British Library Cataloguing-in-Publication Data
A catalogue record for this book is available on request from the British Library.

ISBN 978-1-0685744-2-9

Acknowledgments

Many thanks to the following publications for first printing these poems or a similar version -

"There is an Alabaster Trunk"
"I am Inventing the Story of my Life"
Haight Ashbury Literary Journal

"She had a crowbar and yellow wings"
Staple (England)

"After her release from the state hospital"
Honorable Mention, Allen Ginsberg Poetry Awards
The Paterson Literary Review

"Scalloped Edge of Nothing"
"Parasites Keep Coming In"
'My Mother is a Soft Egg"
North Dakota Quarterly

Contents

Part One *Mother -*
   The Summer of Swamp Rain

My father drank the dark	3
Fountains	5
I've always loved patty cake	6
Scalloped edge of nothing	8
They always danced for you	11
You can buckle your shirt	13
It was gargantuan	14
I have a violet landscape	15

Part Two *Daughter-*
   My Mother's Frog Shoes

You can cast around forever	19
I always wanted a way to take off	20
The dalmatians painted on the curb	22
My mother is a soft egg	24
Did they dance back then	25

Part Three - *Mother -*
   I am Looking for
   Something Elastic

Personal Statement	31
There is fear	33
I am stirring my skirts	34
There is something I'm looking for	35

I want to make a vow	37
I refuse to believe	39
You sing, *You make my heart swoon*	40
There is an alabaster trunk	41

Part Four - *Daughter* - My Mama Swooped Up Everything

The first time we visit her	45
Daisy ate green algae back then	48
It was 1957, for God's sake	51
My mother makes a graveyard	54
When we perch on her hospital bed	55
Not all things anchor with a willing breath	57
Randy is coming soon	60
My mother received eight tulips today	61

Part Five - *Mother* - I Tell the Doctors That Defeat Can Save

I am doing somersaults	67
Everything is a flock of geese …	70
I contemplate my fate	71
They told me it was imperative	75
A Conversation with my Eldest Daughter	76
My sapphire ring gropes my finger	78
Parasites keep coming in	80

They are imposters	82
The nurse tells me	84
They keep talking about me	85
I am separating the peas from the meat	88
My daughter brought me gingersnaps today	90
You marked a red pen over	92
Shhh	94
Feebie says the clothes are starting to dry	95
I finished the crossword puzzle today	97
There are tiny boxes I want from them	99
I can't imagine	102
No one said I could glow in the dark	105
I can't count anymore	107
They are feeding them briny water …	108

Part Six *Daughter - It Was Late August Before My Mama Finally Came Back*

It's hard to tell her she is leaving soon	112
Easter dissolves into summer	114
After her release from the state hospital	116
They did not shave her head	119
My mother made salami sandwiches	120
In the pocket of her skirt	122
It is true there were beetles	124
I can't tell you my mother	126
She had a crowbar and yellow wings	129
I held your deftest skirt	131

Part Seven *Mother -*
    I Have a Peephole of Light

I am inventing the story of my life	135
It is light as a feather	137
I didn't know it would be like this	138
Ceilia says I am stockpiling mercy	139
I am arrested by beauty	141
It won't always be insufferable	142
You have always anointed me	143
It is hard to imagine the planet	144
When you come	146
You wear thin chemise	147
The railroad station holds light	148
You ask for consensus	150
My girlfriend is giving away	151
You impregnated my foot	153
I think I could marry my daughter	155
I don't want to die a frivolous death	157
Nobody will forgive me	158
I have soliloquized want	159

Much madness is divinest Sense –
To a discerning Eye –
Much sense – the starkest Madness –
'Tis the Majority
In this, as all, prevail –
Assent – and you are sane –
Demur –you're straightway dangerous –
And handled with a Chain –
                    Emily Dickinson

The inner fire
is the most important thing
mankind possesses.
                    Edith Södergran

PART ONE

Mother –
The Summer of Swamp Rain

My father drank the dark

out of midnight on the day of my birth
promised to people the world in birds
chronicled lust till it was a seed bed
of my own making.

For seven days he kneaded
and shaped the earth
til it assumed its present dimensions
green on green with innumerable
species of animals leaping
slithering, foraging for
the weight of his fruit.

I woke to delirium.
Forests so thick I could lose
my hands in them.
The sky lit a glow lamp
redtail chattered in the tree
foxglove lent their purple seed
to the wind
children twined pansies.

If there was sin
it was a foreign thing
like those who map anger
on derelict strings.
If the world was destined

to be stockpiled
pinched and pummeled
I knew nothing of that
only the metal chorus of my father's might
my mother's damp voice calling.

The day of my birth was the quiver of
blue bell, chokeberry
the magpie's contrition
when happenstance married
bridal veil, nosegay.
My mother looked out
on the rows of Timothy
flirted with the decent weight
of her fields.
The nurse straightened sheets
boiled water
kept loyal to the newborns
entrusted to her.

I sped to earth
landed with my sopped wings
smooth head dusted in down.
Under the taper lamp's close care
landed ready to bless
be seen here.

Fountains

It was that kind of spring
we sank our feet in, splashed water
pressed bubble gum into balloons
with our tongue's caress.

Jimmy said he could go on forever
missing school, watching frogs
my oldest girl's hair grew past her waist
she wouldn't let me cut it.

It was the April of no lament
the men in our world working machinery
the shops on Hillside three blocks away
with their cash registers thumping.

We exiled the plastic gnome
in favor of hot pink flamencos.
For Mother's Day I got the beach chair
stamped in lemon ices
let my body lounge.

We were buried in fountains I tell you.
All of us threw in good luck pennies
wanted to swoon in the spray forever.
I said *wish hard enough and you will turn
into shiny fish.*
We held hands, squeezed with our eyes shut.
And we did.
Orange pools of them.

I've always loved patty cake

hop scotch
the queen of sisters jack game.
May is the perfect time
for chalking up pavement
playing kick ball
letting the lightening bugs
see you home.

I thought it was nonsense
the need to grow up
get serious about every pale thing
be bolted to machinery
mechanical words
days with a crusty gait.

That was the year
we learned to tap dance -
Jimmy and Samantha, Tilly, and me
found four pairs in various goodwill bins
watched Fred Astaire, Ginger Rogers movies
were given pointers by our neighbor, Betty Lapore
sixty one years old who twice won
the regional tap dance championship
for age 6-12, still had the figure to prove it.

The linoleum sounds better under the tap
of our metal shoes
the counters, cupboards, the cutlery come alive.

Jimmy sports a black top hat
Sammi borrows my fishnet stockings
Tilly practices on stilts with fake cigar, painted lips.

We smell of greasepaint our squirrel stage
stomp, strut, spin
practice our fancy footwork
bury life's sadness
with the *thump thump thump*
of our heels.

Scalloped edge of nothing

that's what your father called you
because of your size
because of the way you shrank from things
set up your sentinel of armies
hid from the wind.

It was the summer of too much rain.
The garden swamped with it
our peonies buckling
the nasturtium barely able to open
their orange lids to the sky.

I was going crazy in that house.
You remember it.
I walked the floorboards back and forth
baked upside down cakes
till the refrigerator was piled with them.
Everybody begging hot dogs
with so much peach upside down cake
on the shelf.

Grandpa died that summer
overweight and in his 40's
heart gave out along with his temper
and grandma had to sell the big house
because he'd never believed in life insurance
took to cleaning doctor's offices
moved into the cramped apartment

slept on her fancy sofa, never bought a bed
shopped at Butners, designed her own clothes.

It's scary the way some things leave us
fall apart
while other things we barely love
stick to us like hot glue
insist they will never migrate.

I smoked so many cigarettes that summer
I though the color of the walls
would turn brown.
Your father aired out the rooms every night.

I wanted the sun back, a blue wade pool
patio with a decent hibachi
man who knew how to use it
wonder how many things get shrunken
before they rise.

It's the summer you put your pointer finger
in the blade of the parlor fan
almost ended up with a stub
the summer I burnt toast
your brother sped down the dump hill
on his two wheeler, busted his left arm
the summer it rained and rained
your dad working two jobs, attending night college
the high humidity

my rayon dresses all steamy
me dreaming the ocean, families with cars
iced tea in glasses so tall you never get thirsty

the day offering up advertisements
of sexy women in red convertibles
ice cream, lovemaking
children who float with me
instead of lagging behind
create their own fantasies
yank the neon flamencos out of our lawn
ride them till we are a thousand miles away.

It was the summer of swamp rain.
What could we do but roller coaster our days
looking for heaven?

They always danced for you

in the cousins' kitchen
kicked off heels, stepped on toes, giggled
Frank Sinatra, Patty Cline playing
our paper cups of cheap wine
the little ones shooting marbles
toppling lines of dominoes on the back porch.

You're always kissing your cousin I'd say
the cousin with the stamp of summer on her face
who years later would end up tethered to a man
that slaughters chickens, stomps in big boots
maps mucky prints across her floor.

It was the summer of 1956
you were eight years old
already stretching the season's green dress
begging the older cousins to look
their hands filled with plates of sauerkraut
sausage, potato salad from Celeste's.

It was a time when life didn't stir windstorms
the day staked to nothing but what we brought
you are the one playing on the stereo
the stench of cigars
the screen door's in and out baneful
the sound of the neighbor's hose
drowning of beetroot, gladiola
the last of the coffee, crumb cake

you asleep in my arms
dreaming of the cousins dancing
the lilt of their yellow and blue skirts
the sky torched with our cigarettes
girls with nothing we needed to do or save
just the gliding, the stomp
the up and down slide of our shoes.

Already you were a mistress
of lemon cake
the world's rapt sermons
things others would later forget
that I would incise in you.

You can buckle your shirt

velcro and bind
keep busy as a yard mill
I have grown used to you like that
detonating emotion
having a certain method for each thing
keeping that stalwart eye on the seasons
what must get accomplished here.

Come spring crows return to the trees
rise up, flutter, land at random intervals.
They make a mockery out of precision
stay active late night
in the clear eye of their scavenging
awning the sky
a missionary of nuns calling.

I am wearing fuchsia
detest the way your hands move
believe that crows signal death
a slouching off of things in our bed

I am wearing fuchsia, sinful
will rise up one day
a profusion of wings in the tree
watch you hose our path
scour your hands
resist the messiness
I stir up in you.

It was gargantuan

the silk heart, velvet roadways
litter of dark covered cherries.

I was afraid I would grow fat
on your words
chocolate catacombs
as if words have a weight
sound that impregnates
insects the grass
leaves children barely breathing.

May still lurks behind the corner store.
The garden iris a host of stubby stalks
in search of sun.

It has been months since I demolished
the cherries, buried the cardboard heart
in the back of a closet crowded with boxes.
I watch the surety of you
way you prostrate beetles
nail railroad ties over the mud lip of our yard
decide where things will, will not be placed
leap over the sweet slumber of my bed.

At night outside the window
possum keep pawing.
They dine on our trash
are hurried by nothing
except the sound of the dogs.

I have a violet landscape

to live in.
Not soot anointed.
You can barely manage
to climb the necessary steps
to my bed.

But that doesn't matter.
It is August
when the heat
beats down on us
all sorts of diseases
are introduced into cattle.

Our baby will be born
in a week, maybe two.
We are screwing together cubbies
crib legs
applying giraffe decals
to the orange wall.

I am still hopeful
of what will become of me.

Part Two

Daughter -
My Mother's Frog Shoes

You can cast around forever

in my mother's frog shoes
they have orange tongues under a green lid
eat algae, bugs
lounge in the world's boggy
have kept her almost incorruptible
while the dark teases.

Don't make me go in I beg
as she drags my body into the pond
bribes me to learn amphibian
sink or swim by my own juices.
I am afraid I will drown
inside her chastened eye, yellow tint
that gobbles debris
sand toys, men.

My mother is the color of longing
what gets spent, what gets left for dead.
Come nightfall nobody listens
place more than a perfunctory ear to her voice.

You can cast around forever
in my mother's frog shoes.
Become stillborn
pregnant in contaminated water
never impose prison
onto the fate
that's been ascribed to you.

I always wanted a way to take off

rise above the gravity of things.
Some people get stuck in glass houses
must martyr the rain
become a cemetery speckled with
plastic roses.

When dining needles invaded
our front stoop
we kept distance
called out to our mother
called out for the night
with its guard of squat kisses.

That summer my mother made me wear
petal pushers two sizes too small
they were seersucker, pink
meant for another girl.
I climb the slope of her stoop
and still remember blue ices
her painted toe nails
pageboy bobbing with an easy lilt.

You will be famous someday
she'd tell me
while she was buffing her toes

looking at the Travel column
wondering where's her man.

But her words weren't for me, not really
the halogen lights and camphor.
They were for the missing beauty
the one who strode down the steps
one February in a season of regret
never came back.

I don't like dice rolls
unearned celebrity
people who are convinced the world
is just what we make of it
never admit to partiality
the imposters in our bed.

Sometimes what we are is not
who we become
the young girl dodging dining needles
grows up to dodge men
mealy dinner plates
the world with its cut glass imperatives
squeezes time, the drab day
into her own volition
the seam of her wrists
not celebrity bound
but still seeded in voile and cinquefoil
the risen color of her own
deft deliberations.

The dalmatians painted on the curb

are not for me
they are for the girls next door
the ones who never need to stew
in cramped shoes
only genuflect to the sweet hum
of the day's hold.

It is March. Pungent with Lent.
I want to be pregnant with possibility
rise up as part of god's love
walk into Easter service
with an anchor of crocus, tulips
atop my head.

My mother has cut my brother's pants legs
just above his shoes
bought me a straw hat circled in blue ribbon
closets my father's strict love
till we are a breakfast of fried egg, bacon
Sunday mass with altar boys, incense.

It is the year before the world falls apart
the vanished litter of kittens
before my mother's loose hands
will be strapped to an armchair
before I start wielding can openers
sauce panning our meals.

My father is still intent over the prospect
of baked ham for the Easter dinner
hot biscuits, mashed potato, gravy.
There are pastel painted eggs
for the morning yard hunt
my mother has prepared for us.

At the Easter table
I keep my wants pinned in my blouse
deny seconds, deny hope
let my father's harsh eye
stand guard over the gravy.

Afterwards, my mother peels out of her pretty dress
sponges dishes, roast pans, plates
till in a few more months we will no longer find her
and all the upside down cakes in the world
will always taste of her lost peaches
the jars of forgotten fruit
she sliced, preserved for us.

My mother is a soft egg

with a dark yolk
fields my life
in spring clover
black gum boots
manages to turn the other cheek
not be openly formidable
back talk the rain.

My mother warns me
not to crowd fate
stab the peonies in my yard
set up a garden
that turns disfigured.

Maybe I am the wish fulfillment
that lives in her side pocket
the aberrant child
the one who decides to have her cake
eat it too

the lemon icing of it
way it curses a small plate
reinvents kittens
mines the yard for lost marbles
paw prints, pregnant wishes
that go hackneyed
in the rain.

Did they dance back then

that first night in the Crystal Ballroom
or straddle the side wall
did she like the uniformed height of him
his lieutenant badges, shock of gold hair?

Was she a temptress with her high heels
low scooped rayon, sleek pageboy
rhinestone rings?

Did they dance close or arm's length
did he try not to step on her toes
learn quickly what he would later forget
did he whisper sweet nothings
talk about his sodden childhood, dead mother
blue orphanage
did she comfort him, soft sooth
spoon him stories of Cape Cod, clam digging
want to save
did he promise forever, a posting in Germany
vow to always care
or was that weeks later
before the deployment
her black cocktail wedding dress
the chalet and maid service in Bavaria
her kid leather gloves
a few years later the news of a first baby

the state side cramped apartment
the two jobs, too many bills?

It was the Second World War.
He held the past of a drunken father, strict nuns
no bicycle, too many schools.
Eventually her swimmer's arms, love of horses
would not save her.
They will be crammed in the apartment
of a three family house
with tiny rooms, a basement bed
whittle the love that had been seeded.

My brother, my sister, and I will carry their knots
like twisted rope
marry our days to too much cake
frayed upholstery
the weight of defeat
that damns up windows
damps down the rain.

But what we become is more than a busted hinge
more than my mother desperately gluing
her borders of gold scroll
across the top lip of our black walls
more than the yard hose's insistent fury
flooded geranium.

I will grow up stapled to god's thin wrist
a season of birds flocking

the gift of knowing that what we lose
can come back
as the determination of cedar
sky's incessant longing
yellow wings in the tree

I will learn that nothing
is impossible
with the wide gate
of our true breath.

Part Three

Mother -
I am Looking for
Something Elastic

Personal Statement

The pocket of my skirt
pools a crop of corn
pigeons feasting
as if it is their last supper.
I sweep floor
stumble into strange rooms.

The Yulpa bird rears her young
for twenty years before they fly.
Nobody thinks strange of it.
They are nursed on electrified milk.

If the day be long then you must
sometimes ride a dwarf pony.
My mother said that
dug hope out of our side yard
knew about the rough and smooth
peonies that must clung
to the night's paupers.

I am looking for something elastic
something that moves past brokenness
with deft refrain.

There are trumpet flowers waving forever
with their pale petaled faces

they hawk poison in their sleeve
make every blind insect their prey
remind me that beauty alone won't save.

I once pricked my finger
slept for one hundred years
slept with worms, beetles
bits of metal in my head
learned never to grow old
became a glass box that jewels heaven
a cleft of light pebbled with strangers.

I hear the Yulpa bird call
want to navigate the sodden world
am willing to portage the wide umbrella
of the rain's weeping.

There is fear

that lives in me
makes for uneasy lovemaking
legs with slumped fishnet stockings
a collision of shoes.

It is hard to see disaster pinned
to polished words
watch the slaughter of things
be reduced to a speck of dirt
spread over the day's road
not worry myself about tired classrooms
the way my husband kerosenes beetles
watches them squirm to death
in the name of might.

I could grow pearl mouthed
not appraise anything
swim only in crisp paisley
never admit to the rain
hem of a woman's summer dress bleeding.

Please don't ask me to peril
what is moist in me
trophy what amounts to chaff
in our fields of grain.

Hummingbirds flirt
at my red orb of feeder
sip furiously
harbor no treachery or distain.

I am stirring my skirts

getting them to respond
lemon taffeta over German lace
my black bra silky under the tank top.

You could voodoo a doll
try to destroy me
but my body will still bounce back
sure as a carnival game
fluff endowed animal.

What do men want
surely not sugar water?
Bite too hard
you might lose a tooth in this world
end up with rock candy.

My husband wants me to come and go
by the slavish chord of his needs
likes me lean as a licorice stick
wants to pour himself over me
as if I don't have a mind of my own
original thought lurking.

I am stirring my skirts
will set fire to my life soon
but nobody knows that
the final privilege of a being
to harbor her own flame.

There is something I'm looking for

in the toe end of my shoes
something that stutters
the language of birds
eludes me like so many men
the heaviness of the hour
purse's silk lining
hidden under a leather sheath.

I want to say I am more
than these crucibles
more than the way money stalks
more than stones in my shoes
the uninvited lecture.

February won't skip on tiptoe
is dispossessed by the rain.
Every window sill
a damp swell of wood
rain smacked glass
tiresome soliloquies.

Be mine I say to no one
to the dog next door
the rinse water's clawing stain
this man I've married who stays
welded to the world's shrewd lips.

I am fragile as a glass jar
the god who loves brokenness
glued back pieces

the eye that must swallow lament
make a cake.

I want to make a vow

to never grow old
be the field cleared of stone
map my hands with so much tender
the birds won't ever be slaughtered.

April wants to stand out naked
in the rain.
I peel back paint
finger the cracks beneath.
My lemon sundress cradles
a communion wafer
my love for you
hangs down to my knees.
I am tired of money.
All afternoon the porch swing
sits sad on its old hinges.
I want to sanctify the earth
rename our birthright.

You swim in a harbor of blue ink
my love for you.
I lull in your stasis
watch the scotch broom, wind
carry the lust of fireweed
replant the yard.

Is it hazardous to save
my best hazelnuts for you

listen with a deft ear
watch the sun impregnate the trees
the field mice's benevolence
want to skate on ice so thick
the pond will always carry me?

Summer will come
scorch my skin, wage war
on my sheerest nylons
dye my hands the violet stain
of blackberries.

I want to stay loyal
burn bright as the beach fire
you can toss your debris in.
Be easy on the eye
steady as the love
I keep safe for you.

I refuse to believe

the world is only a box with strings
my body must move unperturbed
under the weight
of the puppeteer's imposition.

Does anybody want
an untamed lawn
woman with her nails cropped
unimaginable landscapes?

My children draw ladybugs
a hairy dragon
sun with a glued grin
invite the afternoons to speak.

If I empty the house
will god send milkweed
muddle the dark
tease that fulcrum of hope
I've been begging?

You sing *You make my heart swoon*

and my heart swoons.
I want high heels
that silk dress with the crème trim
want to be kissed silly.

In a world of tragedies
nobody wants me to go on
counting petals
crooning to every soupy love song.
I remember the young girl
who hived red beetles
lopsided food
coins of chocolate.

Yellow envelopes of prairie flowers
climb my wall's blank face.
Nobody else sees them but you.

There is an alabaster trunk

in the courtyard
it is the ledge for kittens
a host for the spattered markings of birds
untimely epistles.

Inside I have saved my life for you
cut out paper dalmatians
a smattering of lace
worship that comes from exorcizing tyrants

have saved you lemons
bitter before the sweetness
and johnny cakes, molasses suzies
food with children's names attached.
What we marry is what we save.

You will be courted by stories
that slip inside fortune cookies
help you look beyond the world's derision
traffic light's blank stare

will be my last word
the power of inexactitude
day's handy seamstress
who turns all my loose threads
into a loop of skirt
watches
as I move out of the room's tight fist
into your garden's twirling.

PART FOUR

Daughter -
My Mama Swoop Up Everything

The first time we visit her

the walls are bare
her bed pressed into a bland alcove
That Old Black Magic playing nowhere
down the hall.

My father has brought a cheap box of candy
rung of daisies
my mother fingers them with limp hands.
We are told to stay only half an hour
she tires easily.

My mother is worried about getting fat
the bed tray with its mashed potato
canned peas
flat way her hair looks
asks my dad to bring makeup
a magazine that can travel her to Naples
views of the sea.

The next visit my father brings
a rolled up copy of Good Housekeeping.
My sister and I unload her blush
mascara, fuchsia lipstick
a pair of charcoal stockings.

The nurse tells us she needs time
not a lot of pressure
wants us to talk about nice things

no complaints.
My father grumbles about overtime
at the post office, the way the new neighbor
parks his Chevy at our curb
hoards the space in front of the house.

My mother applies the berry stained blush
bobs hair, puckers her lips
fingers her wrist while my father talks
says she hopes the cold weather will ease
asks for a record player or radio
pair of high heels
worries her housecoat weighs too much
harbors a host of dead birds.

When we leave that day
my father buys us pepperoni pizza
says we must share one slice
because my mother is costing us
a bundle with her hospital bed.
I notice his face is taut, intractable
as the plastic he staples in place
over our parlor windows.
On the subway ride home he barely speaks

just says we better be good
draw something to cheer her up
nothing excitable.

On Saturday the next week, my father
picks out and bags her sanest things.
Says no record player or radio
will travel on the subway.
We arrive with ice cream, her cotton sneakers
a magazine loaded with Easter recipes
baby chicks.

My father says *you are still looking good.*
She wants to believe him
wants to believe not all things perish
in the light we barely ascribe to them.

Daisy ate green algae back then

loved girls with pinwheels, petal pushers
wild hair, a surplus of breath
became my mother's best friend
the summer she moved to Queens.
It was before my brother and sister
before the sludge water and heat lightening.
Somebody needed to violet the stories
my mother pressed like delicate petals
out of her head.

In August Daisy and my mother strutted
arm in arm down the beach
with their skimpy swimsuits, bronzed skin.
I stayed behind, anchored the blanket, cooler
nibbled cookies.
They swore someday they would open their
own shop devoted to crazies, sell rainbow ices
faux fur, Houdini kits
lucky rings that turn the heart frostless.

Ten years later
my mother goes into the hospital
with her cosseted body
skin pale as tapioca, unsteady legs.
Daisy drives in from Hartford
with an armload of zinnia.
My mother fears she's grown sappy
hides herself for a moment under the sheets

notices Daisy's mink stole, its shape, sheen
wonders what it takes to keep the body so silken
it can drown in the world's lust like plump mango.
Daisy smiles, says she can't stay long
needs to hit the road back to
Connecticut before the rush.

For three summers Daisy was
my mother's best friend
till the broader world caught up
the unadulterated devotion
of an ambitious man claimed her.
My mother stayed in Queens
in the three family cramped apartment
cargoed her canvasses, tubes of paint
strapped herself to lunchboxes
a foldout bed in the basement
to cheap sand chairs
versions of paradise that slide down your throat
colored our walls the black of dissolution's tail.

Some love grows thin without enough weight.
My mother asks the nurse to bring blue ices.
The nurse goes out but won't find any.
I want to imagine the world as a decent place

a father who isn't gone all the time
the moon undisguised in my mother's face.

When Daisy says goodbye
everybody up and down the hall
notices her drop dead gorgeous body
platinum hair, silk sheath, saunter.
My mother is wearing her hospital gown
frog slippers
doesn't yet know the bloated
weight of the scale
has learned no real mission
to seize what she can here.
Twice daily she takes her pills
swallows them straight down
the muted slope
of her throat's beckoning.

It was 1957, for God's sake

she was 32 years old
eye turning in her low cut dress
patent leather heels.
Come Sunday morning when she
walked up the church aisle
every man came alive in the
lightning rod of her hallelujahs.
My mama swooped up everything
like a bouquet from god calling
consecrated the custard éclairs
black and white glazed cookies
we bought after church service
to pamper my father's blue voice.

It was before the black parlor walls
string bean suppers
when April still arrived a profusion of tulips
we wore new Easter clothes, hid eggs
planted her sling chair out front
in the middle of the grass.

It was 1957.
The state hospital hadn't received bad press.
They said it was the safest place to bring her.
For her own good.
The long sleeved top she arrived in
barely concealing her wrist's desertion.

She kept wanting a cigarette
her dead father from Plymouth
Santorini's pizza, light on the cheese.

I don't believe god wears armor
goes around sweeping dirt
planting steel fisted cosmos.
Some things manage to stay here
with a deft face
make a pack out of nothing.
Some things get born and then die.
My mother had already buried her father
two dogs, a litter of stillborn kittens
already let her paintings, cargo trunks
slip into a city of dust.

My father claims she has legs to beat the band
makes a decent lasagna
when she puts her mind to it
stops going berserk
with her sideways imagination.

At first we visit on Thursday and Saturdays.
My father tells us she's heavily sedated
don't expect much

we settle for jokes about the weather
the subway ride, the framed picture of us kids.
My mama notices how I barely fit into my clothes
my sister's hair sticks up.

The nurse says it was a good visit
she'll see us at the weekend
don't worry if my mother's fussing
better to keep her hands busy
then sit hour after hour terrified
of going perishing in the rain.

On Saturday my father forgets
my mom's sketchbook
brings a pack of plastic knitting needles
three skeins of dull yarn
dumps them onto the bed.
I wonder what she'll do
with the thick autumnal colors
he has laid.

My mother makes a graveyard

of our roses, pricks what is left
of their parched petals
with the fingernail of her thumb.

We visit often the first few months
bring our book reports, crayoned lady bugs
make everything seem singsong.
She tears open the candy bar my dad hands her
splits it in five, passes a small piece to each of us
slips my little sister the same sticky note
at the end of each visit
the one that says *remember the birds*.

I grow chubby that winter
don't fit into my round collared blouses
hoard crème wafers
rescue them from the terrible fate
of being anonymous in the cupboard.

My mama says the meds are making her bloated
the nurses won't allow her to wear sheer stockings
under the housecoat.
My father claims she looks good anyway
that by Easter she'll be back coloring eggs
hiding a basket we'll hunt for in the backyard.
She says she isn't sure she can function
without a pair of new glasses
ones with a crop of rhinestones
colored frame.

When we perch on her hospital bed

we want to believe we are special
the birds attest to our devotion
every purple and yellow crocus
is a gift from her mind's imagining
to keep us steady until the day.

She's wearing her rings again
a jangle of bracelets
asking to walk the ward
the grounds
watch the trumpet swans preening.

I do not tell her there is no pond
no trumpet swans
just a highway that circles
a ring road, a shopping plaza
too many stores.

My mother is starting to rise up on tiptoe
I can see it in her bid for velvet
the popsicles she asks us to bring
rocket rainbows of color
she licks with a rhythmic thirst.

We talk about school
Tilly's award for the spelling bee
my last report card
the way dad has rigged the ping pong table

back up in the garage
how she'll be coming home soon
we'll blow up balloons, fold laundry
dust the sideboard, make devil's food cake
set her beach chair
in a circle of shade
under our one birch tree.

I'm not sure my mother has heard
anything we've said
tells us the birds are setting off for Peru
their long journey south
that we should scatter crumbs
offer up a host of kisses.

What kind of sloped chair is it she asks.
Is the canvas stripped or paisley
pea green, almost military or hot mauve?
I say *mauve, of course.*
My mother relaxes into her bed sheets
calculates the days behind her
how many are left ahead
how many months of sun come May
the sky will grant her
how many months before the rain
the grey start spitting.

Not all things anchor with a willing breath

My mother is jiving to Frank Sinatra
way out beyond the stars.
We love to watch her lose herself
in the sheen of her body
the way she clothes her past in
gypsy linen, silver beads.

That's what we remember about her.
The doctor wants more.
When did we start seeing changes.
Who gets you ready, cooks meals, walks
you to school, bathes and beds you
as if my mother is an unstable room
that might buckle under our weight.
You have been absent fourteen times
from school this year. Tell me what that's about.

I explain my sore throats, the splinter in my toe
my brother's bad cough, do not say
my mother has been missing us
hates hearing about me being made fun of
hates us stuck for hours at our desks
the photocopied identical work sheets
sometimes wants us to hive with her
invite the honeybees.
They won't understand, I know that.
Her duty is to do what everybody else does.

I say *my mother is always dependable*
say nothing about the playacting
the giant dahlias, late night black paint
she washes over our parlor walls.

Do you miss her right now?
I want to tell him our house is a shell
with no meat in it
that everything we have ever loved
has been whittled away.
I stay calm, say what he wants from me.
My mother is a good person.
We love her very much.
My father works two jobs and goes to night college.
It's hard for him when she's not there.
My mother knows how to hold many things together
stickpin the rain.

Not all of this is true
but he doesn't need to know that.
He is looking for dissonance
cracks in the wall
the plate glass window with pits.

Who cares if my mother burns omelets
my white slip
loathes clotheslines, sinks with dishes

barely has any interest in being a cook.
There are other things some of us are heir to
other ambitions that keep us hinged to heaven.
Rare filigrees.
Things that can go bust or drown.

My mother once wanted to staple the sun
to her tongue, but it drowned
now her nights are a basket of longing
tears of regret.

I want to tell him -
look how she rakes up banished stars
for our bed
pitchforks the terrible certainty
we lend things
in a world of calm scrutiny
sings.

Randy is coming soon

He is the old boyfriend.
The stuntman she married when she was nineteen.
My daddy says it's about time they got to meet
and I know it's not going to be easy for anyone.
We're not sure how he heard about her
after all these years.
When he comes I am supposed to
take my brother and sister down the hall
to the soda machines, stay scarce.

He's from my mother's other life
worked in films
probably was an expert at surviving
plane crashes, cattle stampedes, folded cars.
She shocked the German relations
with her secret marriage
then headed out west with him.
Later, it was annulled, and my mother
moved back to New York City
dragged her cargo trunks, satin gowns
canvases and paint, riding jacket, spike heels
into my Aunt Bertha's duplex.

I am daydreaming Randy
is some prince charming
handsome, swift on his feet.
That his smile can melt ice ponds.
He is more legend than any real man.

My mother received eight tulips today

They were foil wrapped
her first announcement of spring.
We arrive to find a dangle of silver bracelets
tidied hair, turned down bed sheets.
She wants a scavenger hunt
chocolate bunny, jelly beans, floral sheets
the stubby nosed sheen of April
crocus in her bed.

My mother is in a good mood.
Even my father's face looks decent.
She notices my hair has grown
my sister needs new shoes.
Says she wants to stop eating cafeteria food
fried potato, dead carcass of chicken
wants to slim down once she gets out
ride horses.

I try to imagine this
my mother with her dark green
corduroy riding jacket
high leather boots from fifteen years back.
They were part of that other life in Massachusetts
before her marriage to the film stuntman
then the annulment
before my father's military ticket to Bavaria

the birth of kids, no car, a pint sized apartment
lead in her shoes.

My mother is convinced she will start riding again
lifeguard her summers back on Cape Cod.
Says she doesn't want us to stay inland anymore.
She is reminded that we live in Queens.
My father knows of no subway that leads
to a horse stable.
That what she needs is to keep busy
get her job back at Gertz Department Store
pull weeds, patch the cracked linoleum
keep us from bickering.

My mother reminds him that tree houses
are the answer to many a cramped space.
They are not hard to build.
Some remnant wood, a bit of thatching
ratan mats, a slab of foam to sleep on.
My father has turned off his ears
gets annoyed at her impracticality
says he has overtime next week
our penmanship is going to hell
there's only so much homework
he can help with, so many hours to a day.

I don't tell her dad is a tight fuse
ready to break, that his pinched lips

won't ever hijack the moon.
We want to be a happy family.

My brother and sister and I want
my mother to get well
succor us in the three family house
mind the rocks that bury our throats
till we can't speak
never invite over anybody.

In the dark I know my mother's eyes
are iridescent as the wings of a dragonfly
she sees past what others miss
can proposition secret stars
with the fuchsia deliverance
of her hands.

My father has stamped the world's
terrible weight to his shoulders.
Stumbles around with a flashlight.
Cannot see in the dark.
Wants my mother to be waiting.
But she imagines foil wrapped eggs
baby chicks, a dance hall
Easter risen as rabbits in the grass
god's rapt hand
that sees through all folly
raises her up
up
past the rain.

Part Five

Mother -
I Try to Tell the Doctors
That Defeat Can Save

I am doing somersaults

in the hall
entertaining the hospital guests
with my monologues
Judy Garland impersonation
want to turn this place into a stable
where something obscene
unangular can find a home.

The nurses look on
harbor their polite distain
humor me with grey potions
colored pills
that nightmare the dark
believe that everything has a diagnosis
my past will rise up
eyelid the canker in the world's bleeding.

It is spring
I am supposed to go home by September
at least that's what they say
if I behave, act nice
am not the sodden, aberrant parishioner
in a church with straight walls.

On Saturdays, I pray in the chapel
with the devoted, the distracted, slumped over
stroke glass beads
wait for the black and white cookies to arrive.

Don't believe god will save me
the thorny stern one who never laughs
just stickpins my body's plush voice.

I am a lonely chord on a stripped clothesline
can't expect the world to notice
not in a place where only the big
get a throne
am not sure why my husband wants me to be
indomitable but small
a gravel pit peopled with ants climbing.

My children call me their *best seashell*
when they need something
want me to anchor the moon
bribe the nurse to bring mint wafers
cartons of milk.
Anyway, I need to be sedated now
crisp cotton and neat hair clips.

Tell me - if the world is a circus act, blue operetta
if I can reinvent myself anytime
today - discreet librarian
tomorrow - conference consultant, wedding planner
sex siren, celebrity, politician
apprentice of the dark calling

if it's true what the magazines say -
that we are a continent of possibilities
can go anywhere
be anyone

then why do the doctors cast their
most disparaging eye on me?

Everything is a flock of geese with their Heads chopped off

I try to tell the doctor that
defeat saves us
what gets slaughtered here
can never just be shot gunned away
god keeps an ambulatory eye
on the roses.

He makes notes
fastidious on lined paper
only half appears to be listening
shrouds his body in grey flannel
a Rolex watch
the accouterments that success breeds

asks me how I *feel about things*
things, what things
the ridicule my daughter's extra weight will cost
my son's eyes blunted with trivia
the way my husband plastic wraps
the windows meticulous
tosses yard beetles into a metal can
watches them squirm to death
in a pool of kerosene.

I contemplate my fate

nobody wants me to
as if I've been scissored
and they want me to stay this way
the doctors with their white coats
way of scouring the world clean
as if adjustment is the kitchen sink
with a compliant drain.

I am sick of clean
its riotless nature.
Maybe poverty needs me
like the wolf's piercing cry
his hunger that chalks the dark.
Maybe it is only the bird pecked
the mealy mouthed
the torn enveloped
foul stenched
that need us in the end
maybe all our years of schooling
are only practice for this -
to aid what gets forgotten, lost here.

If I scrape my eyes
clean with a sharp razor
will I see the world less angular
will the ghetto be dwarfed
by the moon

the tightrope acrobats
go home to a kinder bed?

My husband claims doctors know
all kinds of things
are trained in answers
I need to be is the good listener
obedient.

Only the nurse shows me
the lack of fortitude of her loose skin
sagging bun that's half fallen.
I know she snatches cigarette breaks
outside the break room
her clothes reek.

Why do I crave what everyone
says I can't have?
There are rules here
what time I get up, dress, bathe
when the breakfast tray enters.
I'm told to keep my hands busy
not with men's pants
but stamping out scarves, baby booties
cramming words into crossword boxes
till I am pasted back

a woman with x-ray vision
who can see past the rain.

My daughter says the school lunches
are cardboard with fake cheese.
I keep telling her father I feel helpless
when she talks about them.
My son's eyes prefer gazing at football
than studying the uneven composure of a face.
My youngest daughter wants to paint the
moon on her wall, says the colors escape.

I have trespassed on god's lawn.
One morning I tell the doctor this.
He is older than his unlined face suggests
asks me what I found there.
A riot of unruly grass, the hazard
of shade growing
swallows no longer stick pinned
In the lawn with plastic heads
You can stockpile a certain kind of happiness
but can't make everybody drink from it.
He seems tired of my proclamations
puts down his pen.
Says *Claire, we'll continue this tomorrow.*
I feel like a suitcase being shut

pawn of this man who decides what is pertinent
what gets pronounced dead.

I am escorted back to my room.
Last week Tilly brought me a night light
with coral wings.
The walls are so smooth and square
you could almost run down the side of them
in a cardboard box, not scab your knees.

The crocus in the squat pot
on the windowsill looks sad.
I spray it with water. Recite poems.
Finally dig it up, wrap it in a wet towel
under my sheet
coax it to grow as well
as it can with a lack of dirt
only the mealy eye of night calling.

They told me it was imperative

to move past the late hour
the cat box with its half anointed wanderings.
After that we set up shop in the tool shed
made love under the moon's sickled tail
tried to remember our life
the whims of it before children
a penitentiary of walls.

April and the fields fused to foxglove
no longer barren of god's love.
I could lounge forever
pamper the clover's red tongue
invite the raspberry shoots into my bed.

Life is never just a corridor of bent leaves.
Even my father knew that
went on anointing the first buds of iris
with his red eyes
put aside his wife's dying lament.

Can we dig up anything
under the afternoon's loose gaze
old shoes, vows, marbles
the rabbit forgotten under the porch
our kisses, their flame and honey
candle and calamine
relearn the cows as holy
the trees as gift?

A Conversation with my Eldest Daughter

Don't say anything
not a word
this is just between the two of us.
A few cigarettes to keep your mama
from lonely
in return a story about Helsinki
night stars admitting an inferno.
We will bag potato latke
sire snow
trace the moon with our fingertips.

We are friends you and me
almost sisters
already I confide all my heart.
I am making great strides
doing just what everyone asks
no willfulness my dear
just abeyance
which is what your father needs.
I know. I know it is difficult
polishing his shoes
making him feel like a big cashew
in a grunt bowl of olives
but you'll be glad you did
that's how you'll fly out of here.

Keeping secret will save you from dissolution.
No handcuffed wrists lashed to the wall.

Europe, that's the future I see.
You'll need a good college, those grades
will turn out to be handy someday.
I'll fly over, meet you by the Louvre
the day a light breeze
your body slim
gracious in the ivory trench coat
long hair streaked under a wool cap.
You'll barely recognize me.
I'll have my good legs back.
My painter's hands, way with men.
Modigliani calling me out of that other life.
We'll hold hands, wander the streets
duck into a Montmartre bistro
share wine, camembert, pate.
You'll recount your utterly incredible life
I'll hang on by the edge of my seat
the way I've become used to doing
later slide off on my own
into the crisp afternoon air
amid dark eyed strangers
remember the way life can take hold
not as shrink wrap from a small roll
but palpable
all our good luck coins tingling.

My sapphire ring gropes my finger

has grown small, unholy
snug in the space between happiness
sits as a remnant of love's chaste skin.

When the equinox comes
I will probably still be here
holding hot coals in my palm
pacifying the nurses
remembering you with braided hair
unafraid to lay your body down in the river
our basket of hard rolls, Myetha's cheese
olives from Cyprio.

Was it o.k. to worship love back then
lathe it on my body
till I was slick, oil spun, shimmering?
You offered me a box, slim silver bracelet
later I lost the stump of my right heel
we wandered the hills blind.
You the shy suitor, skirt caked in mud
my voice finding its way among
your coneflowers, timothy.

I will not be at equinox this year.
Have become blue as the sapphire
a spare coat
the mind the world forgets

that my ineffability clings to.
Please remember me as more
than this brush and comb
the calamity of these bed sheets.

Parasites keep coming in

I've told the nurse about it
they never seem to get enough
are drunk on the nectar of my skin.

I need to move I tell her.
She says they only infest what invites
that I must be stalwart, stopgap the rain
send them packing
with the crumbs of my tray.

I grow steely
resist their assault
pile crumbs into a bug hill
let them wander the miraculous
send them off with a stout talking to
rubber band parade
ceremonial sermon iced in wedding cake.

Over time they become a willing congregation
take their pew diligently by the altar
never fuss or foam
spread disease over my room's sinful.

The nurses turn smugly satisfied
over my ability to take initiative
find the Houdini.
It is not long before I can master hat tricks
resurrect panties, red carnations, rabbits

recover the stolen ace
jello escaped from my dessert tray.

With my slight of hand, new vocation
I'll soon be able to disappear through walls
gather better food from the kitchen
shatter glass with the weight of my words
realign my past
till it tumbles back painterly
hot tempered
a season of schoolgirl lust
burning.

(State Hospital, N.Y. 1957)

They are imposters

candidates for another world
no campfire would let their
carcass roast.

I bribe the cook to keep their
dead bodies off my plate
but he doesn't listen
insists on presenting me with
bird wing, pork chop
leg of the chicken
body of god disguised with gravy.

It is dangerous what they are
up to in here
dicing up animal parts
fancying them up with parsley
piped potato
pudding as fake and lemon
as the world wants.

I could be meringue
whipped for the pie

a piece of leftover
the forgotten eye of the pig.

They keep feeding me
as if dead things can enervate
help me claim water
rabbits
be a follies dancer
girl in the subway counting stares.

There are imposters here
marauding as meatloaf
a girl's best friend.
I refuse to dine on them.
They are the cup of gall
Jesus drank from.

All day long the nurses paddle
in and out of my room
with their crisp white uniforms
even disposition.
Is it true that nothing frightens them?

The nurse tells me

I look *gorgeous*
to stop fidgeting with my hair.
Men have always loved me beyond reason
wanted to pin me to a room of their own making
watch me squirm.

My husband has dyed my body the color of exile
sends black beetles
to conscript the plush of my bed
fake furs the love I keep for you.

It takes hours for me to hoist myself up
out of the pale sheets, blanket's dead weight.
Through the window new leaves
March breaking through winter's regret
with blind crocus.

I want to shed this housecoat
stalk the trees naked
shock those neighbors who judge
tell my doctor there is nothing wrong with me
god peeps in every window
will never let me vanish.

They keep talking about me

the nurses with their stout bodies
chaste hair, orthopedic shoes
don't let me rest
claim I sneak cigarettes
am too pithy, high minded
turn my back on the bland dinner
like a princess.

I refuse to kneel to their petty gods
be piped icing on a sickening dessert cake
enamel my nails, tease hair, scribble notes
pitchfork the day's calendar

remember my father's shrill hands
the dead weight of his yard daisies
lilacs trailed by a stern voice
the way we make a diagnosis
chicken wire madness
turn what is aberrant, inspired
into insipid as rain
want a world with easy stride
no complexity.

All morning I plot my discharge
memorize what they do and don't want to hear
hang my words on a perfumed fence.

My cyclone settles down to a backyard purr
I comb hair, scour lips, smooth robe
straighten the bed sheets.

The nurses begin to smile
satisfied to see me do what they want
make myself a thin recipe, voiceless altar.
In five weeks from now the doctors will
convince themselves that I am purged
no longer crush pills
stake out an alter kingdom under the bed sheets.
I earn a few privileges
can sit out on a bench, drink in the first tulips
marvel how the grass wills itself up
through hard dirt after bare bone winter
the frilly collars of the daffodils tease.

If the room here looks drab, lifeless
with its bald walls, reductionist scenery
maybe you have only yourself to blame.
There's a secret altar some girls must live by.
It is carved out of the despair of our wrists
out of tired homilies, aberrant kisses.
It holds a barnyard of children, indigent ponies
must make scarcity pass for more than it is.
I am impregnated with neglected rooms.

To roam my geography is to taste the salvation
of pear trees.

The hospital has high walls beyond the footpath
barbwires the night
keeps time in its head immutable
doesn't want the god of pinwheels
to climb my tree
plant strange birds of paradise.

They don't realize there are
already translucent beetles in my bed
that nobody needs a flashlight in the dark
only an altar so hidden, durable
it can sidestep the rain
turn every creature into something more
a willing wet grave.

I am separating the peas from the meat

the way you can separate thoughts
divide rainwater
lick the ice cream away from the stick.

It is Saturday
the day they will come
my daughter stocky in her tight jumper
my son lisping
the littlest one glued to her bear.

I have promised I will be good
look my husband straight in the eye
not disrupt him with anything
from this other world.

I have been trying to stickpin fancy
to my metal bed
imagine what Tilly's dolls would
think of hanging out here
all dressed with no place to go
the peas always wanting to roll away
from the plate on the tray table.

Life here doesn't roll away
it sits safe, stockpiled.
My hands grip the bed
but my will lets me go anywhere -
Nairobi, the Grand Canyon

Majorca, New Orleans.
I don't want to become
a plastic version of myself
tar pitched woman.

They are coming today.
The nurse clears away my tray table
says I need to start eating more.
I have spared the peas
the meat with its whole heart, legs missing.
Will live on bread and water if I must
fasting being a royal road to spy god
lure you irrevocably into the lonely
cavern of my bed.

My daughter brought me gingersnaps today

remembered how I love them
knee high to my father when he first
placed each brittle morsel onto my lips.
Kids remember such strange things.
I only told her once about it.
After all, my big burly father died
before she was born.

My oldest daughter, the born pleaser.
I'm afraid she'll give too much
more then gingersnaps
wield her fractured heart
and then what will become of her.
She is a miser for angel cake
sneaks plates of it between meals.

For years people have mistaken me
for her slim older sister
the one in cotton petal pushers
who splashes the rain.

Is it cruel to remind her that men want
a thin stick, the rhapsodic voice calling

that what's only skin deep
can sometimes save?

I try to tell her that there's a certain
kind of baiting the world wants
plush as velvet, spiny as high heels
that we are asked to slide down men's throats
like a stick of blue ice
shimmer and melt, but never
truly give ourselves away.

You marked a red pen over

my fallen margins
controversial half ends
made your definitive statement
as if there was a failure in being equivocal
my blue pen pausing to listen to the lisp
rat a tat tat
of the world's loose curves.

I have stopped writing letters on paper
pronouncing myself in easy fistfuls.
They are a bastardization under your scythe gaze.
You make me march in a straight line
shoot darts from a spired roof.
I cataract the light
till I can hold any dark thing

The blue line of the dungarees drying
on the clothesline
slope like so many ducks
laid out on a practiced pond.
A man's shooting range has many faces.

Where did you learn to aim like that?
As if every one of them needs to be dead center.
I am dead center.
Not that you can see me anymore.

Peeked in my froth coat
frog slippers
I look at you slant from inside my bed.

You have brought roses, almost a dozen
so crimson no one can see their thorns.
I've never liked the scent, color of hybrid roses
almost indecent how they devour you
before you drown
but I graciously sport appreciation.
Someone else can arrange them
when you leave.

I'm going to survive here
waddle and quack
make a mockery out of sin
stand in the rain till I am so porous
grass grows up through my skin.

It is hard to locate the center of things
spot the red-tailed hawk mining the dark
walk your way through madness
with a complacent hand.

My body was not shaped for disaster.
The erasure of trees.
Will my scars matter to the eye of god
who sees past all complaint
never lets the faltering ones
stand out forever
empty.

Shhh

she tells me to go to sleep
stop asking for things
removes the tray table
draws the pale curtains
as if only silence can speak.

Am I never allowed
to be the unruly child
the maple tree's wood seat
rapturous in the April of its swinging?

Every visit my husband eyes me
with his superfluous grin
smudge marks my homilies.
I don't want to perish
don't want to be needless
only my husband's desire for cake
the pumped up of his ball field.

How many times have I sipped
midnight from an open grave
imagined the world cracked open
no more erasure, price to pay
hysterical voice.

In the dark I knead
not tired old bread
but this other life that keeps
stalking me.

Feebie says the clothes are starting to dry

stiff as cardboard on the back line
that the neighbor family stays busy
nursing four kittens.
I want to be sprinkled from a yellow
watering can, soak the earth
not feel soiled
stranded under a curtain.

In spring I want to dangle
my feet off the dock
slush my lips with pond water
blue ices
soft serve cones with a heap of sprinkles
forget the diligence it takes
to sidestep winter.

My husband is anticipating Easter
brought me a new cotton dress.
It clings like the tight skin of an orange
was meant for another woman
someone with shrunken hips
even spaced crocus.

This morning I pocketed crusts of bread
asked the nurse for a glass milk jug
want to lure guppies
let them temporarily swim

in my jug as miracle
am afraid of the horseshoe crabs
that crawl in at low tide
might bite.

When I was a child my mother's swimmer arms
always took her out past the boats.
She made a habit of entering the water
waving goodbye
the gardenias on her black swimsuit
stabbed with light.
From the shore my sister and I
watched half afraid.

Not every beach has perfect shells
fluted scallop fans without chips.
I used to spend hours gathering
what others shun
imagining myself maneuverable
tied to a decent rudder, sturdy sail
skimming through the bay
beyond the rundown bungalows
patios with portable card tables
a raised flag
past my mother's rhythmic arms
out to where the swells lift and eddy
the waves can finally carry me.

I finished the crossword puzzle today

managed to find the word *peripheral*
slot it in the far boxes that run down the page.
This last space filled in with the non-essential.
It seems fitting it should end like this
testament to the affability of things
how calm we can be
even slumped in a stiff chair
with no tangible future.

They say I'll be home by September
just in time for my thirty-third birthday
newly plump and not too pasty
ready to gather the lawns' play toys
water the wilted begonia
calculate the weight of his shirts.

My daughter says she's planning a party
will skip the Barbie cake laced in pink
settle for my favorite devil's food chocolate.
I suggest an icing of fuchsia peonies
tell her to feel free to underestimate my age
plant three candles and an oddball extra for luck.
Tilly says the summer is almost over
I'll have to hurry if I want a ride to the beach.

I finished the puzzle today.
But I already told you that.
It was stubby fingered, black and white

like the newspaper columns.
I can lay it to rest.
They will be pleased with me
setting my mind to something tangible
seeing it through.
My husband prizes a capable mind
precise words.

I have vowed to be different
more discerning, tidy
clear in my new itinerary
able to map the route to strange cities
keep the peripheral shadows from
overtaking.

I can see our apartment, its crisp curtains
crew-cut lawn
everybody on a diet
my mother rising up from her grave
appalled at the sinister baker
my crème puff longings
the way I cleave to every cake
their sheer determination
to make their icing anointed faces
known to me.

There are tiny boxes I want from them

foil wrapped and ribbon twined
not huge whale bones
not three layer cakes with
an inch of icing.

It is my birthday tomorrow.
I turn thirty three.
Have spent years trying to figure out
how to live, store up the levity in things.
Burn more omelets than my husband cares to know
am diligent at conversing with trees, frogs, poems
feathering fans of bamboo
twining ropes into a lack of henchmen.

My oldest daughter will grow up different
from the rest.
I already know that about her.
Her penchant for fallenness
the hours of playing alone.
She has an eye that sees past entropy
and into another day
will need a suitcase of magic tricks
sympathetic god towing.

Not all things turn out lemon ice
in a thin rain
learn how to speak for us.
There are people in this life

locked up forever in a small suitcase
who probably never find a feast day
lover's hold that is decent
they are the windows the world forgets
their view is out past potted plants
cropped lawns
and into a century of rain.

In a little while I will pass through
the screen door that divides things.
Scramble eggs, box lunch meat
help my children keep a thread of hope
while my husband crew-cuts the yard.
He is like a rock tumbler
covets only polished stones
jasper, onyx, topaz
grinds off their pock mocked faces.

In my pocket are raw amethysts
before the jeweler claims them
magic tricks only my kids see.
Sometimes white rabbits get
yanked out of my hair
the woman who appears to be sawn in half
crawls out whole from the box.
I turn up the queen of hearts
three times in a row

not in real life but in this one
the one I've created out of folktales
fairy slipper
midnight's flirty fleece.

I have become the consummate magician.
Watch the bed table
how it rises up in thin air
see if you can detect
the slight of hand in me.

I can't imagine

I will really get out of here
break through my past
be rolls royced in style through the gate
my fake muff trailing.

My husband believes there's a cure
to every ailment.
The doctors assure him of this.
A dab of oil here, wrench there
and everything falls back in place
becomes solid.
You have to learn to walk before
you can run.
When we learn how to run will we find
it useless as sin pawing?
Nobody talks about such things.
The impatiens slow opening
fur infused buds of the magnolia
way god's toes managed to lift tender
onto water after the boat fled.
I am expected to be a worshiper
of prudent spaceships, never vagrant
disarming in my blue kimono.

In August the world makes a commotion
out of automobiles
the sun merciless on their metal tops
the steering wheel hot as hell

and our hands peeling.
They snug roadways, gather in drones
remind me of the life I'm supposed to be living
places my children never get taken.

I am safe from them in here
and in my backyard.
Safe to keep my slim wrist bracelets singing
deft dreams of another world.
You can curse your life
or set up a plan to claim it.
I have been known to be devious
written my sister for a train ticket
back up to New England
back to Plymouth where the tall ships
are as big as my childhood
my suitcases, children towing
German relations a gaggle of gossip
welcoming me back
incredulous to see me
after the escapade in New York
annulled marriage to my handsome stuntman
two years living in the chalet in Bavaria
my husband's ex-military, basic brown shoes.

I'm not sure anyone really knows
the power invested in me.
I am alive in paisley, pastel heels

my summer legs floating
my paints and canvas, blue inked notebooks
pillbox hats without the pills.
Arrive like honey fresh from the hive.

Are we always rowing toward Eden
always the thrust and pause of it.
Jubilation you've heard of that word.
My sister and I once knew it
snapping lima beans in our aunt's back garden
searching sand dollars on the beach
our sandals with their perforated toes.
The days seemed so long then.
Unweary, loose.
They were carried on henchless clotheslines
on bits of ribbon, jump rope, twig.

Joanie, get me a train ticket home.
To Boston. I can take the bus from there.
On the first train possible...
Will there be any lifeguard jobs
open this summer?
Is the waterfront already busy?
I hope not.
I only want to see the ocean.
Has the south cape changed much
and the salt stained wind
heaving shape of the sand?

No one said I could glow in the dark

but it seemed a worthy occupation
like ice cubes lifting up lemon water
stars that flashlight sin
bleed the night's blue hold
pregnant wanderings.

I practice secretly
sit up loose in bed
allow a certain disposition to take hold
one that eludes names, conclusions
makes me the piper of
no one's particular homilies.

The doctors are unconvinced
of the light I harbor
see me as ill formed, misshapen
a product of wobbly imaginings
want to stuff me in box
marked *sensible*.

There are places you can go
when there is no room
lights that come on in the dark
blind things
my x-ray vision that sees through walls
clutches the courtyard's damp tongue.

Does anyone want us to glow in the dark
find a tunnel through the world's treasons?

The doctor claims the world runs on reason
not fig trees, voluptuous fruit.
He has a crisp white shirt, cashmere jacket
soldiers his words into a stiff regime.
But I do not intend to be here forever
humor his official hold
pilot my words like a serpent
will navigate his dark
wait to shed my skin only
in the forgotten grass
with the moon gleaming.

I can't count anymore

not like my children do
on the even-ruled lines
they use in the heft
of classrooms.

The world is a coat
with too many buttons.
It fastens so tight
we exile the rain.

My husband views thrift as holy
a way to cough drop the wind
corral birds
sermon god till we
hold ourselves back –
the birthday present
that never comes

wants me to turn sensible
eat the meat
chemically altered food on my tray
compliment everyone
be the soft spoken mite
grateful.

I smooth clothes, sponge my body
say the *please* and *thank you* others expect
never constipate the light they swear by
their stringed boxes
learn to eat with a judicious spoon.

They are feeding them briny water
moldy oats

my horses with their beautiful manes.
I enter the field naked
gather vetch
squander the sugar cubes, sliced apple
the nurses have left on the tray.

My horses never cower at my touch
purse their lips as if the envelope
of happiness must kneel.

It is almost autumn.
Almost time for farewells
moving back home.
We have no stable to keep them.
Just a border of iris
ping pong table, rutted garage.

It is hard to see horses
so boney their spines ache
watch them move lethargic
across the field
summon their delicacy to
a landscape of scant grass.

My children are growing up
without ponies.
I am afraid they will squander
their lives

become technicians with suction shoes
spend their day screen gazing.

They are feeding my horses
briny water
a mush of old oats, timothy
as if they don't know better
as if you can sedate what you deny
their stark scrawny thinness
ankles turned wobbly as stilts.

I have bribed the hospital cook
for more oats, sugar cubes
their worm tinged apples.

My doctor shakes his head
over the angels I see slumped in the tree
the parasitic mornings
children without periwinkles
just iodine cake.

He has no real idea
what the world itself
invents in me.

Part Six

Daughter -

My Mama Swooped Up Everything

It's hard to tell her she is leaving soon

that the release date is pressed in clean folds.
My father has already vacuumed, lugged groceries
lined our pantry with the hope
of what will soon be sanctified.

My mother's hands are scalloped shells
with an ocean missing.
She no longer paddles down the hall
can saunter easy now, toss her hair
claims it's the garden that cured her
not the doctors with their pills.

My father tells her she needs to respect
the work that's been done
reminds how she could barely talk
when he first brought her in.

She claims -*Everyone confuses things*
dismisses the fool as dim
nakedness as a cracked jar
instead of a tribute to
god's lack of savagery calling.

My father doesn't know what to say
talks about missed handball games
my brother's lost tooth

the browned out grass
black spot killing our roses.

My mother plays the fortune teller
gathers the pale of my father's hands
notes their size and pith
predicts he can do many things with them
crush a lipstick, beer cans, build a rose arbor
succor a child, beehive
coax the rainwater to speak.

We giggle as he pulls them away
and my mother forecasts our long lives
says my brother will outlive baseball stadiums
that my sister will be loved by a secret admirer
I will carry a rare flower in my heart.

I imagine my father's hands
worth more than his orphaned childhood
the columns of numbers he rattles away
imagine him conducting an orchestra
smoothing the length of my mother's hair.

Already I know for years to come
my mother will be a half disguised gypsy
want to rumba, eventually forget how
that my father will continue to
plastic wrap our windows
with the firm of his fists.

Easter dissolves into summer

it is late August before my mama
finally comes back
leaves the hospital in a cotton shift
so long, stiff it shows nothing of her legs.
Her arms look bloated, skin white, pasty.
My dad has shoved her things into a cheap suitcase.

It doesn't seem fair to plunk her down
right in the middle of us
with the new school year starting
my little sister struggling with her inhaler
my brother begging for Cub Scouts.

At first she returns to burning things –
omelets, hot dogs, meatballs
forgets the value of watches
spends long minutes gazing out the window
sketches tulips and peonies
plans for wilding the yard.
Keep an easy way with her
my father tells us
no use setting her into a commotion of birds.

My sister and I iron, dust
stop arguing over who has to make the lunch
vow never to get sick

watch mama clip her nails so short they bleed
dye her hair butterscotch
so the light of the sun turns friend.

The first few months our neighbors
keep their distance
watch her jam in neon flamingos
sit out in the rain showers, chain-smoke.
November she starts keeping us out of school
sends notes about Tilly's sore throat
my skinned knee, Jimmy's attack of measles.
Nobody seems bothered.
My mama gone past the black parlor walls
burial ground of dwarf carrots, potato.
She pyres herself to the trees
lets us anoint our bodies
in metal garbage cans, cardboard boxes
spackle, mud, paint

reminds us she has decided
to stick around
not go off ballistic to heaven
leave us stranded
in a *shithole house*
pistol polished
without soul.

After her release from the state hospital

It is almost a disaster
seeing my mother in the billowing pink
the way the neighbors look on.
She waters the bands of peony
drowns them in puddles
that flood the path.

My father has no patience
is sick of canned soup, baked beans
blackened omelets tossed on his plate
denies my mother the sacrament of night candy
makes her screen the moon from their bed
curtain the room black
so he can sleep better.

All autumn my sister, brother, and I
hover on tiptoe
play alone under the single tree.
The nuns at the Immaculate Conception School
send home brown packages that pile up.
My mother barely pries herself loose
past the clothesline
chain smoke of her cigarettes
narrow band of our yard.

I am elected to the school color guard that year.
The teachers grow impatient with my
yellowed blouse collars, unspectacular shoes

say my mother ought to do
something about them
that holding up the flag on stage
for the Friday assembly is an honor
should mean more than a tight jumper
wrinkled sleeves.

My mother tries ironing
burns my one slip, melts my beige skirt
til it shrivels up on the board
uses bleach to brighten my blouses
smiles, says -
soon you'll be so sunny
you'll frighten the rain.

There are envelopes you can reserve for heaven
my mother has a whole fist of them
they puddle in her dresser drawer
are penned in blue ink, curled gothic letters.
I don't know yet that one day
I will work hard to decipher them
that after she dies, I will inherit
her mother of pearl sideboard
cargo trunk of paintings
cute rayon dresses, faux leopard muff

the drawers full of god's broken homilies
don't know yet that no man wants
a passionate woman with a river of scars trickling
that sometimes flame can smolder in
all the wrong places before it ignites.

My mother lights her cigarettes one after another
as if dying can be a work of art
act of treason
momentary stasis
her one clear act of defiance
in the face of my father's distain.

They did not shave her head

what happened to Sylvia Plath
does not happen to my mother.
She returns to make meatloaf
Jello, potato casseroles
dab paint on ornate eggs
becomes the bird with wings too ungainly
in a country of merchants.
My mother learns to deny the big plate
live on the slimmed down version
of happiness
in which we are trained

chirps with the birds in the tree
invents a pigmy name
for the splashy of sunflowers
never abandons hope
just paper banners it to our fence
sinks her feet in mud
lets them swim there
as if hope is something murky
you embrace with your whole body
her feet wet, clotted in muck
squishing and squirming
in our yard puddles
mapping them into
some tabernacle for home.

My mother made salami sandwiches

with yellow cheese
peach upside down cake
began to wander the house
in the same flaming kimono
both summer and winter.

On her fortieth birthday we gathered towels
took the long bus ride out to the beach.
Her paisley swimsuit barely fit
we ate candied apples
my father bought her a windsock
with a short tail.

She hadn't died yet
was still packing lunch boxes
trying to content herself with the shop job
spike heeling her past, the time in the hospital
so it wouldn't rumble.

I'm not going to tell you
her hair turned prematurely grey
there was no more riot in her
that my father learned to forgive
her burnt toast, meatloaf
content his hands with the fiery
passion of her ways.

Over time I learned about pitchforks
the secret woman vocalists stashed in her bag
tired clotheslines
women with suede shoes
St. Jude medals
who martyr the wind
have a hard time staying alive
about fires so banked you can
barely get a marshmallow
to ooze in their flame.

My mother pasted paper hearts to my chest
invisible ones
stapled my father's bald eye raking the roses
the world's hidden ranch houses
chickens on hooks with their necks broken
death calling with its dampest wing.

All morning I sip tea
look back on her love, whittled life
the way it wound around jump ropes
gift boxes
my stretched neck
till I could hardly speak
didn't know how to be here, save her
a mute bird on a sloped clothesline
my sweetest sounds buried.

In the pocket of her skirt

I find pigeons flying
an intricately tiled room
strange stories.
The zabago nurse their young
for twenty years on capulta milk
of the imprego tree
before they are slowly weaned
from the nest.

I press my ear close
dine on her electrified milk
uneven words.
Hey, do you remember the moth game?
Capture a moth, then let it go.
Don't hurt its wings.
Remember
if the truth be told then the shoe fits.

My mother wears holes in her hands
straddles the night's worn thighs
is looking for something elastic
that moves past brokenness
with an honest face.

There are trumpet flowers waving forever
with their fluted horns, crème petal face.
They hide poison in their sleeves

make every blind
unsuspecting insect their prey.

I find it remarkable that words can wear
such disguise and thunder
pitch indecency, pain
to beauty's snug waist.

She pricked her finger
slept for a hundred years.
In sleeping was reborn again.
Even the glass cage couldn't hold her.

Everything alights from a swept room
grave that keeps reinventing itself
beyond the worn face of his thistle.

It is true there were beetles

kerosened to death inside the Chock Full of Nuts
coffee cans in our yard
it is true my father looked on unperturbed
never seemed to sully his heart.

He strung up pole beans, sprayed weed
pruned rose bushes
grew plump tomatoes for my mother's salad
anchored his anger to the rake of leaves, bugs
devotion his children withheld from him.

I am the product of what couldn't be born here
the aphids that persisted on our palest peonies
mud puddles that gullied the rain
longed to hide
harbor fingers anchored to daisies.

I comb the night looking
for my father's bald head
want to move past the light bulb of him
way he purged what he might have prized

am the lilacs he clipped in April
tucked in bud vase on the side table
am the crushed dreams he walked
into his forties with
the dismissed jobs
strict orphanage, dead mother

alcoholic dad
defeats that claimed him.

I am the flashlight that sees in the dark
sets up a strange moon
round and full as the life that was meant for him
round as my mother's gorgeous body
that bent over forwards and backwards
till it fled
and he was motherless again
not knowing how to look for the heaven
I have needed to find for him.

I can't tell you my mother

had a happy life
knew what it was to be worshiped
lull in a porch rocker
wander through the gold-spun
mercy of the fields

but she kept a light burning
beeswax and her own volition
stumbled through secret doors
with sequined rooms waiting.

She didn't know how to edge a lawn
iron men's shirts
keep the past
close to her like a tiny bird
that needs sheltering
sang French cabaret tunes
wore red stilettos two sizes too big.

My mother stalked goodwill bins
made upside down cake
rang a brass bell into the room's sleepless
held envelopes seeded in cranes
an uneven past
deft inheritance.

I have seen her cut corners
skirt buildings, paint portraits of women

burn the even hem of my slip.
If she was a loose stone
aberrant bride
disaster waiting to happen
should we condemn her
her inability to wrestle with the world's fleet feet
make her walk a straight plank
into her children's classrooms
condemn her as poison, treason
a juicy peach on a rotting stem
incarcerated train wreck
sex siren, lusty polisher of ripe men's floors
the minuet on a dimmed dance floor

will she come out reformed -
the dutiful citizen, t.v. watcher, politician
incontestable office worker, clothes sorter
juggler of hundreds of thousands of things
shaped and buffed and redeemed into something
other than the sovereign of her own light
be kitchen cleansed, a deft stream
of the world's love for money
abbreviation of her body's most sultry pose

was I the abortion of some grand plan
that never found its place

was I her daughter or the mother watching after her
the dream that never happened
or the life that is about to set sail

will I die of contentment
be the worshiper of my mother's thin veil
the chronicler of what remains
what gets taken away here
will I slip into my mother's dress
be the defiant act against reason
spike heel bridges
hold the yellow envelope
of her love high above
the tragedy of the world's raking?

She had a crowbar and yellow wings

if diphtheria or the plague
ever hit us she would have been
the avenging sister.

I count my life by the way
she painted my days
one burgundy dab at a time
messy and tissue loaded
till eventually I was a fire truck
shiny apple
girl with red bandanas
waving her way around truck stop exits
retreating armies of forsythia.

My mother cast no weighty
aspersions on the world.
She was not a senator, a sex kitten
consumer of our fondest inventions
wore her bracelets slippery
a silver jangle, family of twirling gypsies
till newsmen held their breath at her sight
and even the seeded rye loaves
on the shelf at Reitman's Bakery
rose twice their height beyond
the yeast consecrated to them.

My mother was never able to divert wars
bring home soldiers, stop the oil drilling

save cows, pigs, chickens from factory maul
lay the lasagna flat and even
damp press my father's clothes
make him guileless
banish the sinister in honor
of her throne.

If she crowbarred some triumph over
the seasons of our lament
it is only for us to tell
the pith of her hands
uncrumble of hard soil
vaulted pantries
men's zippers
the scour of what gets paved.

But it was her vulnerable
I liked best
the way she waved her wings
into the afternoon shadows
hoisted her skirt
twirled in yellow chiffon
staked the love of her children
till we became circus acrobats
blue gentian
frogs that morph into princes and queens
thorns ground into her crown.

I held your deftest skirt

neither sank nor swam
hovered as if the damp night might hold me
its star incised moonlight
decrepit love songs, spiky heels
that walk over the constellations
in a bid to find you.

There are choirs in the dark
muffled voices
children with limbs missing who
still manage to skate the pond
women with decent weight
camouflaged happiness
who must stickpin in place
the love they once knew.

Cut loose the threads someone whispers.
I am tired of so many commands
the strict nature of my days
the dress hem's call for mercy under
the sterling gaze of the scissor.

Everything loosens after that.
No longer hovering
I mount the stair.
Snow pillows the trees, the lawn
coats my hands in this other devotion
of my own foresting.

Part Seven

Mother -
I Have a Peephole of Light

I am inventing the story of my life

scissor and paste like a jigsaw to which
only the skilled can lend their complacency.
Loose headlines collide with missing skirts
yarrow, the abandoned shed
winter's white pasty knees.

Everyone in my family stopped believing
the future would become them
ran their fingers along busted keys
became a chorus of the world's confusion.

You don't know this but my life
refuses to fit on a single page
bulges margins, inverts words
makes girls into winged creatures
that fly through the sky's curved hood.

My husband says my life is a soup kitchen
discarded treats, plastic tray table
says I will wake up one day
unable to lip read, memorize bird call
will be glued to my own indecisive.
The radiator will be turned up
the room spiteful.

He claims I will become
the fallen princess

sex kitten siloed away
juggernaut of lunch boxes
cat litter, lined paper.

Little does he know the true palette
of what god intends for me.

It is light as a feather

the road I have constructed
a slab of finely grained wood.
The flutter of my heart, impenetrable.
Something only you can see in the dark.
My scissored hands braying.

Encyclopedic eye that moves
past the curative, the manic
with paint stained hands
moves past your pumped up reason
that makes every word a pedant
tramples the trials of children
scalds what it defends.

I have a peephole of light
spiring my soul.
It drowns in your pedestrian shoes
carefully contained foam.

My mother said apostrophes would save me
their muted wings, lack of definitive
admonished me to listen
keep my skates laced
able to skim over hard surfaces
circle
never need to inscribe death
onto the weight of my blades.

I didn't know it would be like this

always digging my fists
out of a grave
counting
on some kind of stupid luck
to save me.

You deny desertion
come to me
with your loose net
eyelet burning

cast all my
tired aspersions
into the thin corridor
of your gaze.

Ceilia says I am stockpiling mercy

like a pageant queen
who can't get enough.
It is November.
There are dead leaves in the yard.
My children's classrooms breed
a chorus of facts
straight lined desks
lack of recess.

I am planning on a yard sale
sorting what can and can't be given away -
old baseball mitts, stuffed dogs
yellow galoshes, my first prayer book
Aunt Jude's birdbath, uncle's hunting rifle -
it's remarkable what old things
you can resurrect from a basement.

I am doing this in the hazy name of
a winter vacation come February
when the assault of grey strangles.
I have bribed Jerry over at the A&P
to come help sort and tag
stack to make a good appearance.
My husband warns me it makes no sense

to lowball prices so everybody
gets a bargain but us.

There are templates you can keep
in your head reserved as sacred
they are unhampered by the rain
can pogo stick over buildings
glue their soles to any sharp ledge.

I have a set of them
my recipe against disaster
hallmark birthday card
that opens with a voice singing.

Ceilia thinks I make a big thing
out of spare change
the ground's orphaned pennies
have a habit of crowding mercy.
She doesn't want anyone to know
her husband is a stranger
that she hoards too many shoes

doesn't realize that to apostle hope
you must allow for some deft contrition
that it is the unfaltering who commit sin
go around proselytizing goodness
emblem themselves to a holy grail
narrow as the polish on their shoes
beaming.

I am arrested by beauty

but what does the world care
except skin deep
the kind I get from moisturizers
wax totems
whittled weight.

The trees oust birds
they land in my arms
an orange cacophony
despise the fate
we have imposed.

I mine the dark for clues
to summer's vanished dress
paved meadow

mine the surety that lets us
stand out in the rain
porous.

It won't always be insufferable

trying to contain me, turn the pale
of my white wrist in your palm.
Every girl has a map to happiness
penciled somewhere under her breath.

Come morning the field is swollen
with elk grazing.
They skeleton the raspberry shoots
are partial to spring's new growth
stumble off to feed on the orchard.

Have I perjured your faith in me
let my heart sour on a sunken vine?
I know it is not what we take
but what we leave behind
that matters.

You have always anointed me

I am an empress of your seed
want to see past dissolution
the world's crimped sleeves.

One day I won't be painted modest
with a blue veil
stiff as the church pews
nor altar laden with somber priests
good boys dangling their incense
I'll be piquant, fiery even
the dash and stumble and flame
of every alive thing.

I have to whisper all this, of course
or else people think I am hearing voices
talking to myself again
have moved into a diseased room
with tilted elms, teacups
a pregnant daybreak bleeding.

It is hard to imagine the planet

tilts and turns on a slim axis
that every day the sun vanishes
the moon arrives
get crammed down our throat.
But I like the moon.
Italian opera.
Summer ices that never prostate
just sooth our blued lips.

I wonder what it would be like
to be pregnant again
invest myself in a new baby
a being so ripe she can hold
the whole world in her arms
not spit.

My other children are getting older
barely notice the dozing impatiens
pussy buds on the star magnolia
blue bells first green hair coming.
I wander barefoot in the yard.
They no longer follow me
lock themselves behind screens
glass windows
too soon let the metal trellises

of the dying world
adjust the mien of their gate.

My oldest daughter worries
about her weight, angel food cake
good grades so her father will love her.
My son rides mini bikes, ruts out the yard.
My youngest wants to be the popular color
of her friend's yard pool.

If the world is just a shop floor
of fishnet stockings
spike heeled shoes flailing
will I wake up tomorrow dismissed
subwayed inside a life I resent
cram the garden with neon flamencos
glass orbs, an orange sling chair
so that perhaps I can stay
attempt valiantly to stake the moon
to my breath?

Will you recite Keats
gift me with ribbon
remember my wiser words
forgive this fallenness
the way a being
can get reduced to nothing
before she lifts?

When you come

arrive with a ream of poems
ordinary shoes
liquid eyes amid the world's madness
come disrobed
will you invent a new landscape
laden with snow?

When you come
will you come gentle, decent as
the once fallen know how to be
will you bake cake
aspire toward righting shaky windstorms
not need to vandalize the intricate
of my beadwork?

I imagine the two of us then
sopping wet in the field
what we will and will not need
to say to each other.
The impulse to let only our hands speak.
The absolute certainty of joy
as not one more second away.

You wear thin chemise

enter my house with your nails scratching
spill flour across the floor
flatten my daughter's fluff toy
till I can't think clear
almost believe there is no word left
the birds have fled
every day will be a lightning rod
littered with our lack of faith.

Easter begs for a new tablecloth
vinegar and food coloring, chocolate
the chicks protracted cry for being.

I apostle my days to new grass
the forsythia's yellow tongue
imagine what it might be like
to be here
not scarecrow staked, waxen
but indefatigable
augured to your love
letting the dough in the bowl rise up
prove me.

The yellow and red tulips
in half wood barrels by the drive
grown back
erect in this wordless space
I have saved.

The railroad station holds light

the solace of pigeons.
It is hard to move away
pray that someday my words
will find their way back
spider your days
return as a nest in your ear
the leavened lament
of birds calling.

My goodbyes are fractious
as the world's tongue.
I remember my spike heels
the click of them
way the world's weight
drowned the clear joy of my voice
how you stood there
motionless below the train's
metal windows.

No amount of field daisies
can emblem this love
hold it keepsake against the day's
cramped breath.

Be the everlasting
the green stubs beyond ash field
be the limb that cleaves
to the sycamore tree drunk on dew

the lupine's tall breath
ground swell of damp apostles
be the loyal girl loitering
amid the leaves.

You ask for consensus

I congregate with peeled paint
the garden's tomatoes, forsythia
fire engine my wants
stake our beans up on a bamboo pole.

My dowsing rod
is as ancient as the wind
as supple as night calling.
I carry the dark
wild honey of children
refuse to marry a cramped
map of the city
hybrid blooms in a glass house

let you stomp footprints
all over my body
thick as a bride.

My girlfriend is giving away

her only daughter.
She is young and beautiful
willful as the dark.

My friend fashions hope for
her bridal gown
calla lilies to be thrown overboard
when good luck baths.

She will be long and slim
in her heirloom gown.
There will be many pictures taken.
He comes from good stock
works investments
garners above average wage.

My friend tells me they've
already put in an offer
for a house on Long Island
three bedrooms to start
a backyard pool.

I am not terribly interested.
Not because I don't want
to wish her a good life
lusty marriage
career as secure as bank vaults
but because I am fearful of the treatises

we make with the world
their shape, brine, cost
the way our glowing pictures
forecast nothing of the boy
burning insects
the girl with her dreams severed
because decency
turns out to be such a fragile thing
like the blush of roses
the return of the garden's peonies
the fact that what gets saved
what gets spent here
can sometimes come back to haunt
with an egregious wake.

You impregnated my foot

with five toes
impregnated my hands with fingers
that could lust here
stroke a lover's hair
calm children
send out missiles
that bleed blue ink narratives
on yellow rice paper
counter the rain.

I am holding the reins of a life
that doesn't seem to need me
the dilapidation
way we must stay young
rock tumble the wind
be precocious
a success story
unchipped vase.

Can I set my life different
bury the sharp
be a constituency of flame
know that what falls apart
can arrive back
a language of wings?

It is hard to mine the dark
keep a steady eye over the lupine

make sure they don't stumble away
raise the voices of children
as more than a cramped box
mock emblem.

It is June.
You dig out iris
paint the mailbox
promise a palpable summer
undeterred allegiance
the strict measure of not always
receiving what we sow.

I think I could marry my daughter

she doesn't yet disown eyelet
rake the voice of lilacs, peonies
need to crew-cut our yard
plaster ebony over the parlor walls.

I chronicle life in the notebook
I keep for her
its constituency of hungry birds
blue ink
curve balls she catches
with a practiced mitt.

My oldest daughter rambles
around her singular devotions
is not popular
garners few birthday invites
Saturday rendezvouses
but someday someone will notice her
her vague peculiar tenacity
the originality of her wings.
She is a fish on dry rock
a remnant of the ocean's breathe
river's longing.

In the park we escapade
the dull lives god has confined to us
stalk Parisian cafes, nibble good bread
cycle Brittany

spread out our blanket.
I will be old when she turns new again.
Already you can see the child
inside the young woman
devouring angel cake
craven for light.

She will be more than a small shirt
on a tired clothesline
cargo the love I have for her.
I tell her she will not be strangled
will not
will walk into the afternoon shadows
with the trail of her dress swaying
her decent eye holding court over
every drab thing
return to earth everything that has
inadvertently been taken away.

I don't want to die a frivolous death

staked to a lack of faith
sagging empire
that refuses to rust.

I have contemplated nothingness
with a careful mien
disposed of my girth
want to find a handhold so sturdy
it steers past the rain
holds fireweed, blue gentian
the light's least strict gaze.

I don't want to die a frivolous death
be viewed as inconsequential
for that other voice I heard calling
for never climbing the right ladders
of your esteem.

I raise my spoon and I am bite size Alice
antique lace, Emily Dickinson, Neruda
potato casserole, poems, pauper
migrant, mouse.
I am Thoreau's bean field
the maul of the evening news
snowfield in winter
the young girl skating figure eights in the park
boy who will part with almost everything
for the majesty hidden beneath each word
in the hope of something truly sacred.

Nobody will forgive me

for dying early
making the night my lover
stealing a path past loneliness
with spiked heels
the voice's least syrupy homilies.

I wear yellow chiffon
impregnate the dark with so many
peonies the sky turns songbird
traffics in care packages, folly
poets who pass out verse.
The first will resign
the last find their place.

If my voice was once shaky
it now takes on a clear sky
the blaze of fireweed
traffics in losing things.

But then I know it is dangerous
becoming nothing and everything.
Some will detest me
walk by as if I am leper
the imperceptible gnat
dim witted dance queen
never revel in the deft
of my wings.

I have soliloquized want

muddied my life in half spent
fugitives of the page
epistles with shaven light

tethered to thorns
sloped bread, children
the chapel of trees
wait till your voice arrives
to anoint me.

It is April
when my body relearns green
the stretched neck of poppy
fairy kingdoms
the rhubarb wide veined, jubilant
above the weeds' reckless.

It is April
when out of the perilous
the mind's spinning
you populate my field with rabbits
the sky's stage show

it is April
kisses hijack the clothesline
unmangle every mean thing
travel beyond brevity
wild and free.

Toni Thomas lives in Portland, Oregon. Her poems have been published in Austria, Spain, New Zealand, Canada, England, Scotland, and Australia. In the United States her work has appeared in over fifty literary magazines
including *Prairie Schooner, North Dakota Quarterly, Hayden's Ferry Review, the Minnesota Review, Notre Dame Review, Poetry East,* and more. She has been twice nominated for a Pushcart prize, and won several awards. She has published twenty-five collections of poetry and six books for children.

Her figurative clay sculptures have been shown in gallery exhibits in Portland and Chicago, displayed in literary magazines, and housed in private collections in the U.S. and England.

Her short documentary *One of Us* was shown at the Trans-ideology: Nostalgia festival in Berlin and at the Museum of Contemporary Art in Taipei.

Since Toni loves to create and sits buried in reams of poems, manuscripts, clay figures and images….she likes to imagine all of them out in the world swaying wild as the lupine.

tonithomaspoetry.com

www.ingramcontent.com/pod-product-compliance
Lightning Source LLC
Chambersburg PA
CBHW030437010526
44118CB00011B/682